JN410159

달빛에 띄운 연정(戀情)

Love in the Moonlight

정찬우 한·영 대역시집
Poems of Chan-Woo Chung : A New Collection

달빛에 띄운 연정(戀情)

Love in the Moonlight

시 · 정찬우(鄭燦宇)
Written by Chan-Woo Chung; Poet, MBA

번역 · 최홍규(崔鴻圭)
Translated by Hongkyu Choe; Poet, Ph.D.

밀레
Millennium

Rm 210 Seoktap officetel Building
53 gil 18 Hyoryoung-ro Seocho-gu Seoul,
The Republic of Korea
Telephone ; 82-2-588-4671~2
Facsimile ; 82-2-588-4673
E-mail ; hyunwoot@hanmail.net
ISBN ; 978-89-97815-
Price ; USD 15.70 / 20,000Won
Published in July, 25, 2023
Printed in the Republic of Korea

서문

시인이 시를 쓰는 것은 자신의 지적 능력과 상상력을 형상화하는 작업이다. 또한 자신의 투철한 삶의 철학과 사상을 표현함이다. 따라서 시집을 낼 때마다 흡족함 보다는 두려움이 앞선다. 그러함에도 깊고 넓은 인성과 지성의 아름다운 시를 쓰고자 노력하고 있으며 그 시가 세상을 밝혀주기를 소망하고 있다. 나의 시의 중심 주제는 사랑, 겸손, 은혜 그리고 인생의 삶과 세월에 관한 깊은 명상이 깃들어 있다고 하겠다.

이 책은 한·영대역본으로 된 일곱 번째 시집이다. 따라서 두 언어로 대조하여 읽음으로서 상호 보완적 이어서 독자들의 이해와 감성이 더욱 흥미로울 것이다. 나는 한국문학의 세계화를 위하여 40여 년 동안 꾸준히 노력해 왔으며, 이제는 세계인들이 한국문학에 대한 정서를 많이 이해하고 느끼고 공감하고 있음에 그 보람을 크게 느낀다.

이번 시집 역시 중앙대학교 영문학교수 최홍규 박사님께서 원어에 충실한 우아한 문체로 번역에 수고해 주셨다.

지금껏 국내외의 많은 독자들의 호평에 깊은 감사를 드리며, 이번 시집도 흥미롭게 읽어 주시길 기대해 본다.

2023년 7월 10일

서울특별시 서초구 우면산 기슭 의석서재(義石書齋)에서

의석 정찬우(義石 鄭燦宇)

PREFACE

Poem of Philosophy of Life and Thoughts

The poems that I write are to originate from my personality, intellectual ability and imagination. I expresses my thorough philosophy of life and thoughts. Accordingly sometimes I would not be satisfied with my poems. I wish that the beautiful poems of deep and broad human nature and intelligence could be sustainable to brighten the world. I insist upon identifying the growth of aesthetic tint. It is not difficult to point out the central thesis of my poems. It is necessity of the establishment of the value of love, humility, benefit, and meditation of life and time.

This Korean and English book is the 7th bilingual edition. The readers who read a bilingual book can understand better the text. Because different languages are complementary. I steadily make an effort to globalize Korean literature. I am glad that the readers of Korea and foreign countries might read the poems with interest. I genuinely appreciate professor emeritus Hongkyu Augustine Choe who has been The professor of English poetry at Chung-Ang University in Seoul, Korea more than 30 years. Dr. Choe in elegant style has translated all the seven volumes of my collected poems into English.

July, 10, 2023
At the Euiseok Library near the foot of
Mt. Woomyun Seocho-gu Seoul, Korea
Euiseok Chan-Woo Chung, MBA

| 목차 |

제2부

바라보는 것

chapter 2

To Stand and Stare

제3부

하얀 마음

chapter 3

The White Heart

제4부

숲속의 대화

chapter 4

Dialogue in the Forest

제5부

광야

chapter 5

The Open Field

제1부

바람의 세례

Baptism of the Wind

행운을 가져다 준 사람

참으로 아름다운 사람은
진정 가슴이 뜨거운 사람이어요

뜨겁다 못해 눈물이 많고
그도 모자라 자신의 피를 쏟아 부어
남을 치유하는 사람이어요

이 세상
그가 바로 당신이란 걸
당신은 정령 그걸 모른 채
그렇게, 그렇게 아름답게 살고 있고요

당신,
당신이 내 곁에 있다는 건
나의 운명
나의 행운이 아닌가요

The Man Who Brought Me Fortune

You are really beautiful man
Indeed the heart is warm

Not only warm but also tearful
Furthermore you draw blood
Donate the blood to patients who need it

In this world
You are so contributive to others
You are not aware of such good deeds
You live so lovely willingly

That you exist beside me
Is my destiny and fortune.

기분 좋은 사람
— 자화상

미소와 정감이 넘치는
부드럽고 따스한 가슴을 가진
당신은 언제나 기분 좋은 사람입니다

단정한 언어와 품행
깔끔한 성격에
넘치는 카리스마
당신은 언제나 존경의 대상입니다

직선과 직언의 말투에도
겸손과 배려가 묻어나며
유머와 위트로 항상 낮은 자와 함께하는
당신은 진정 행복을 안겨주는 사람입니다

믿음 소망 사랑을
몸소 실행으로 옮겨
뭇 인간의 마음을 사로잡는
당신은 진정 우리들의 로망입니다

The Agreeable Man

— A Self-portrait

Smiling and very emotional
Tender and warm heart
You are always agreeable man

Decent language and conduct
Smart character
Overflowing charisma
We always respect you

The manner of a straight talk
And plain speaking are proportional
To modesty and humility
Young people with humor and wit
You really bring happiness to us

You practice faith, wish and love
You catch the heart of all people
You are really our romance.

그대에게

세월이 약이라 했든가요

잊으려 잊으려 해도
잊혀지지 않는 안타까움
후회한들 무슨 소용 있으랴 만은
되돌아가고픈 사연
그대는 아실련지요

뉘우침과 깨달음에 물들게한
그대의 역사
두 손 모아 무릎 꿇고 회개케 하소서

부모님께 못 다한 효심
못 다한 열정의 삶
하늘을 우러러 종달새처럼 지저귀게 하소서

참된 사랑의 진리
몸소 실천하여
그대가 바라는 삶
후회 없게 하소서

To You My Beloved

It is said that time and tide is a drug

It is unforgettable lamentation
That I try to forget
Although regret is of no use
You might know the state of affairs
Which I wish to go back to the past

Your deep story is repentance and discernment
Let me kneel and repent joining my hands

Unfilial and impassive behavior to parents
Let me warble like larks in the sky

The truth of genuine love
Live up yourself to your beliefs
Don't repent your personal life
Which you wish to be the way of living.

흔적(痕迹)

생명체는 스치는 자리마다
흔적을 남기듯
인생 또한 그러하니 무얼 남길까

잘난 사람 못난 사람
남기고 가져갈 것 많을지 모르나
빈손으로 떠나는 길
흔적이나 남기고 가지

사람은 착하고 악함의 행실을 남기듯
시인은 가슴을 울리는 한 편의 시를
음악가는 감성의 리듬을
화가는 색으로 말하는 그림의 흔적을

삶이란 그렇게 자랑스런 흔적을 남김이 옳지 않은가

Traces

As living things leave traces
At the places passing through
Man also should leave something

For strong man or weak man
There are something to leave
But man passes away with empty hands
Man should lave traces

As man might leave good or bad behavior
Poets could leave poems
That touches the heart
Musicians could leave an emotional rhythm
Artists could leave pictures of saying colors

It might be right
That man should leave such proud traces.

신혼의 꿈

새벽에서 새벽을 잇는 걸음으로
신혼의 단꿈을 쌓던 젊은이들
동분서주 십년 세월
적금과 보험, 증권과 주식으로
오막살이 면할 꿈에
온갖 정성 바쳤으나
이십 평 아파트는 이십년의 세월이네

아들 딸 자녀 양육
유아부터 유학(留學)이니
힘에 눌려 겁을 먹고
무자식이 상팔자란다

선인들의 삶은 정(情)으로 살았건만
젊은이의 삶은 부(富)로만 살라하니
메마른 정서에 꿈 잃은 나그네요
길 잃은 철새란다

하나 알고 둘을 세면
열과 스물이 보일진대
뚜벅 뚜벅 쉬어가며 감성을 길들여
이웃도 나도 너도 돌아보는 지혜를 싹틔워
불꽃을 살라라

The Dream of Honeymoon

Young people worked busily from a dawn
They piled up the dream of honeymoon
For about ten years they were greatly stressed
They accumulated money earnestly
By bank savings, treasury bonds and stocks
To buy their own house
It took twenty years to buy a small apartment

They think over the education
For their children from kindergarten to studying
  abroad
They are afraid of the hard task
They say that no child is the best policy

Ancestors attached importance to affection
Present young people pursue wealth
Their sentiment is dry
They are travelers who lost dreams
They are migratory birds that lost the way

If they know one and count two
They could see ten or twenty
They would steadily walk sensitively
They should take care of neighbors wisely
And display bright blazes.

어느 날

어둠의 빛이 채 가시지 않은
어느 날 새벽
매일처럼 드나드는 산책길에
스산한 추위가 엄습해 온다

완전무장이 무색토록
몸도 마음도 뜬구름으로 방황의 길을 걷고
사색의 뇌리는 먼 산의 어둠만을 응시하는
호젓한 발걸음

삶의 무상과 희열을 감내하는
또 다른 하루를 지새야하는 일상
세상의 넓이와 지상의 깊이로
자유와 진리를 음미하며 오늘을 살아야 한다

후회와 낙담이 없는 시간들
삶의 무게만큼 크기를 가늠하는
저 일상의 하루를 위하여
새로운 나를 세워야 한다

On One day

On One day at nearly dawn
I went for a walk as usual
It was very cold

I protected myself against the cold
Both body and mind wandered as floating clouds
The mind of meditation stared at the dark
mountain
It was a lonesome walking

I feel keenly the transiency and ecstasy of life
It is routine that I spend a new day again
Considering the wide world and
The depth of the earth
Today I should live
Appreciating freedom and truth

In the time neither remorse nor despondency
Taking aim at the weight of living
For the routine day
I should build up myself anew.

바람의 세례

지상엔 흔들림의 여운이 춤을 춘다
바람으로 가슴으로
생각과 뜻의 교차점에서
사랑과 우정의 착각 속에서
권력과 황금의 귀로에서
너도 나도
모두가 바람의 세례를 받는다

사랑이 여물어 꽃이 필 무렵
그토록 따스했던 햇살도
촉촉이 수분을 공급했던 땅거미도
시샘의 바람에 간지럼을 탄다

세상사 흔들림의 원천 속에
오늘도 내일도
심호흡의 세례를 받는다

Baptism of the Wind

The lingering of shaking dance in ground
By wind in the heart
At the intersection of the thoughts and intents
In the illusion of friendship and love
At the homeward way of power and the gold
Both you and me
Everyone receives the baptism of wind

In the time of crops when love blooms the
flowers
Sunshine so warm, it was
The moisture was also moist shade
Tickle in the wind of envy

In the source of vibration of mundane affairs
Today and tomorrow
Take the baptism of a deep breath.

지금 하세요

세상은 내 것도 네 것도 아닌
무형의 존재
그러면서도 어제가 있었고
오늘이 또 내일이 있는 것

허나 시간의 상념은
존재를 무색케 하는 허공이니
내 곁의 진실과 허황된 방황에
겸손과 침묵을 깨고
속 시원한 내성(內省)을 드러내는 것

기회는 언제나 다가오거나 존재치 않으며
후회와 반성의 길 역시 같을 진데
그 길과 존재의 가치를 놓칠 땐
영원한 후회만 남는 것

주어진 기회에
진심을 토해내는 용기 또한
우리들의 몫이니
지금 하세요
내일은 그 진심의 존재가 허상일 것이니

Do Now

The world is neither yours nor mine
It is formless existence
Nevertheless there was yesterday
Also there are today and tomorrow

But the concept of time is vainness
That brings shame to existence
Beside me politeness and silence
Which are broken up by truth
And absurd vagabond
It reveals cool introspection

Chances do not always approach or exist
The way of repentance and reflection are same
If you lose the way and the worth of existence
Only the eternal reflection remains

Take the given chance
The courage of vomiting truth is our portion
Do now
Tomorrow the existence of earnestness
Might be a false image.

허무(1)

내 화려한 날개 넓게 펼치니
벌, 나비, 곤충들
군무를 이루더니

향 잃은 날개 아래
하루살이마저 보이지 않네

뜨눈으로 지샌 지난날의 열정과
반평생 뿌려온 숱한 씨앗들은
가슴에 젖어 은은한 향으로
홀씨 되어 나르고

여가의 낭만을 꿈꾸었던 자는
외로운 지평선에
또 다른 핵을 심고만 있네

Nihility(1)

When I spread out the luxurious wings
Insects of bees, butterflies etc.
Danced in groups

Under the wings without fragrance
Even mayflies are not seen

Passion in the past days when slept little
And many seeds I have sown
During a half century
Warms up my heart
With a subtle perfume
Flies like a spore

The man who dreamed
Leisure and romance
Now sows a different core
In the lonely horizon.

절망의 끝

희망이 없다는 것이 절망이라면
끝이라는 것은 무한대의 미래를 의미하는 것

절망이란 힘겹고 나약함의 근원이라면
희망이란 무한대의 가능성을 의미하는 것

그 양끝을 향해 마지막까지 가본들
끝은 보이지 않고 만질 수도 없다는 것

허약한 마음의 속성이 주는 한계가
끝이라는 걸 사람들은 정녕 모르는가

마음의 끝점을 찍는 순간
고공을 향한 날개가 펄럭이는 것

위든 아래든 양옆의 어디든
그 끝은 내 마음에서 오고
내 마음으로 가는 것

The End of Despair

If hopelessness is despair
End means by endless future

If despair is the cause of weakness
Hope means by endless possibility

Although we go to the last of both ends
We can't see and touch the both ends

Really we don't know that
Faintness is the limit of the both ends

At the moment we put a period of thinking
Wings flutter toward the high sky

Top and bottom or both sides of right and left
The ends come from my heart and go there.

의식의 전환

삶이 버겁다하여
피하려는 자
행운이 넘친다하여
자만과 과욕으로 의시되는 자
시간과 공간의 여백은
사고(思考)와 관념의 상상에 따라
가진 자의 것으로 거듭나는 것

해 묵은 집념
응고된 아집의 끈을 풀어
오는 날을 위한 씨앗으로 묻는다면
비겁지 않은 삶 일진데
뉘라서 그리 어려움만 토해 내는가

먼저 내민 손
먼저 잡는 손
하나가 된다면
소리 없는 아우성의 깃발
창공을 향할 진데
허리 풀고 가슴 풀어
절여진 마음 맑게 흔들어
꿈으로 거듭나는 생(生)의 전환

Change of the Way of Thinking

One who escapes living
That is beyond one's capacity
One who is very happy
Boasts of self-satisfaction and desire
Time and space is reborn rich one
By the way of thought and notion

Old tenacity of purpose
Untie the string of egocentricity
If bury seeds for the future
Living might not be beyond capacity
Who could vomit the difficulty

One shakes hands with other
The soundless flag of crying
Upward the vault of heaven
Untie waist and heart
Purify the dirty heart
The ecstasy of life is reborn through a dream.

단비

먹물로 단장한 옥색 하늘엔
어둠을 뚫는 빗줄기가
목마른 대지를 두들겨 깨운다

주름져 말라버린
갈기갈기 찢기운 몸엔
호흡이 멈춘지 오랜 세월

너로 하여 이루어진
가냘픈 삶
생명으로 돌아올지니
설레이는 꿈이다

얼마나 많은 기다림 속에
그토록 먼 길 돌아 이제야 온 것이더냐
촉촉이 적신 삼라의 가슴
풍요의 기쁨으로 마음껏 호흡 하렴

A Long-awaited Rain

In the blue light sky adorned pitch
In the dark the streaks of rain pour down
Rain awakes the thirsty earth thrashing

Earth has dried and made deep lines
Totally torn earth stopped respiration
A long time has passed since then

You has managed to revive the feeble life
It's a dream of a loudly throbbing heart
That vitality would come back

After really a long waiting
You returned by a roundabout way
Moisten the hearts of all nature
Perspire delightfully enjoying abundance.

빛과 그늘

밝음과 어둠
행복과 불행
단맛과 쓴맛
기쁨과 슬픔은
태초에 한 몸이었다

앞면이 열리면
뒷면이 숨고
뒷면이 웃음지면
앞면이 찡그리는
태초에 한 몸이었다

어찌 하나만을 취하려는
어리석은 인생
흑백의 공존을 모른다 하는가

Light and Shade

Brightness and darkness
Happiness and unhappiness
Sweetness and bitterness
That was oneness
At the beginning of the world

Front side open
Back side hides
Back side smiles
Front side scowles
That was oneness
At the beginning of the world

Why does man adopt only one side
Man is foolish
Why man does not know
The coexistence of blackness and whiteness.

밝음과 어둠
행복과 불행
단맛과 쓴맛
기쁨과 슬픔은
태초에 한 몸이었다

Brightness and darkness
Happiness and unhappiness
Sweetness and bitterness
That was oneness
At the beginning of the world

제2부

바라보는 것

To Stand and Stare

길 찾아 떠난 나그네

먼 옛날, 책 속에 길이 있다기에
큰 길이 무엇이며 작은 길이 어디인지
그 길 찾아 넘나들었던 좁은 공간들

타오르는 불꽃의 향기처럼
손닿는 대로 눈(眼) 속에 먹어 치웠던 습관들
행간을 따라 먹어도 먹어도
목마른 갈증 속에
길(道)이 어디며 덕(德)이 어딘지

태풍에 휩쓸려 몰락해 버린
거대한 일생
죽어버린 언어들의 행렬
평생을 찾아 헤매어도 꼭꼭 숨어
들어내지 않는 진리여,

꿈같은 꽃길 찾아
시들어버린 불꽃 다시 지피면서
그 길 찾아 떠나려 하네
아우야, 아들아 함께 가지 않으렴

A Traveler Departs to Find a Way

Once upon a time and even today
It is said that there is a way in books
What is a wide way?
Where is a narrow way?
Narrow space to find those ways

Like the fragrance of burning flames
The eyes eat up knowledge in books
Also eat up between the lines
But unsatisfactory and hungry
Where are the ways and virtues?

A huge life was perished by a storm
The procession of dead languages
The deeply hidden truth
I can't find it out all my life

I find the way of flower like a dream
I ignite again the extinguished flames
I will depart to find the way
Brother, let's go with my son.

삶의 향기

두 눈을 가리운 채
가슴으로만 느끼는 당신이기에
그대의 눈빛이 아득히 멀어져만 갑니다

어찌 빨려들었는지
그 길이 아픔이고 외로움인줄 알면서도
그저 눈멀고 귀 먹어
헤매일 뿐입니다

풋 내음으로 젖어오는 싱그러움은
신비에 싸여
조용한 파문을 일으키는
그림자가 되어

황량한 메아리로만 들려오는 당신은
내 영혼을 불사르는 삶의 향기입니다

The Fragrance of Living

I close my eyes
Only I feel you in my heart
The light of your eyes is a long way off

I wonder how you have absorbed me
Though I know the way is painful and lonely
I have become blind and deaf
I only stray about you

Freshness from the smell of greens
Has been wrapped in mystery
You have become a shadow
That you silently make ripples

I hear that you echoed back desolately to me
You are the fragrance of living that burns my
soul.

눈물

세월의 무게만큼 눈물이 많아짐은
마음이 여려서도
감성에 젖는 시간이 많아서도
모질지 못한 삶에서도 아니다

한 방울의 눈물 속엔
애환이
또 다른 방울 속엔
숙연함이
방울방울 마다
또 다른 사연들이 뚝뚝 맺혀진다

사랑도 미움도
기쁨도 슬픔도
성취와 실패의 마당에서도
하염없는 사연의 방울들이 뚝뚝 녹아내린다

세월이 주는
아니 삶이 가져다 준
지혜와 감성의 깊은 사랑의 선물이다

Tears

The increase of tears as much as
The weight time and tide
Has no relevance to feeble mind and sense
It is not because of pliable living style

In one drop of tear
There is joy and sorrow
There is solemnity in another drop tear
Every drop of tear contains different matters

Love and hatred
Delight and woe
Success and failure
Absentminded matters drop tears

Through the stream of time and tide
Living brought us valuable gifts
Of love with wisdom and sentiment.

어머, 이걸 어쩌나

난 이미 사랑에 빠졌나봐
눈앞엔 헛것이 보이고
가슴엔 피돌기의 심장이
단거리 선수가 되어 하늘을 날고 있어

헤어짐이 아쉽고 돌아서면 그리워지는
아, 난 이미 사랑의 늪에 빠졌나봐
청춘이 아니었음이 다행일까
아님, 황혼의 이 느낌이 다행이었을까

도덕과 양심 사이에
견우와 직녀로 다리를 놓고
넘어선 안 될 이성 앞에 무릎을 꿇었다네

누굴 위한 선언일까
상처로 돌아올 아픔을 알면서도
후회 없는 정이 그리워 그 길을 가고 싶다

Ah, What Shall I Do?

I might already fall in love
I get improperly seen
The pulse of my heart is flying in the sky
As a sprint runner

After I part from my beloved
I long for her immediately
As I might already fall in love with her
Fortunately I am not young
Or it would be fortunate
That the feeling of an old man

Between morality and conscience
The bridge of the Altair and the vega
I knelt before the other gender
That should not have crossed over

For whom the manifesto is
I know the pain of damage
I would like to go that way
Longing for the sentiment
Without repentance.

이게 아닌데

감각의 끈을 놓은 잊혀진 세월

어느 날
밀물되어 가슴을 헤집더니
출렁출렁 포말 되어 우레를 친다

이게 아닌데
이게 아닌데
이성과 감성의 소리가 엇박자를 친다

세상사 한 번 가는 것
이성의 지배에 감성이 울고
감성의 지배에 이성이 우니
내 마음 갈 곳을 잃어
감성을 따를까 한다

It Embarrasses Me

Forgotten time released the string of sense

One day the inflow of the tide
Scratched my heart
The overflowing bubbles thunder

It embarrasses me
It embarrasses me
The sounds of reason and emotion
Swap crisscrossing beats

Man is mortal
Emotion weeps against reason
Reason weeps against emotion
My heart lost the place where I go to
My heart might follow emotion.

바라보는 것

님은 무언의 침묵으로
바라보고 있다
작가는 물끄러미 서있는
그녀를 화폭에 담고
또 다른 이는 그걸 연주하고
나는 그것들을 음미하고 있다

첩첩이 쌓인 일상의 풍광
이미 일차원이 아닌
삼차원의 세계에서
겹으로 덧칠해진
삶의 굴레

To Stand and Stare

She stands and stares silently
And an artist draws the woman
Who stands and stares
Another sees her and strikes up
I taste all of them

The scenes are heaped with routines
Already it is not one dimension
But three dimensions
The bridle of life
Has been painted twofold.

그리움

바람이 몰고 온 추억 속엔
그리움이 날개 돋아 파도치는데
어쩌란 말이냐 어쩌란 말이냐

내 마음 나도 몰라 갈 곳을 잃어
해와 달이 멍들어 어둠을 깨우지 못하는데
어쩌란 말이냐 어쩌란 말이냐

네 마음이 내 마음이고
내 마음이 곧 네 마음이련만
은빛 산등성으로 밀리고 부서져 격랑을 치는
님이 그리움을 어쩌란 말이냐

애닯다 서글프다
야속한 님이여
정주고 돌아선들 잊을 이 없건만
그 얼굴 보고파 어쩌란 말이냐

Yearning

In the retrospect that wind brought
Yearning waves like wings
What shall I do? What shall I do?

I lost myself where to go
The sun and the moon are bruised
They can't wake up darkness
What shall I do? What shall I do?

Your heart is mine
My heart is yours
Raging waves have swept
The slivery ridge of a mountain
What shall I do for the to you yearning

Heart breaking and sorrowful
Distressing love
You gave me sentiment of pity and went away
I can't forget you
I eagerly wish to see your face
What shall I do?

바람

가슴이 흔들린다
꽉 메어진
비집고 들어갈 곳 없는 그 곳에
바람은 깊숙이 파고들어
조용한 파문을 일으키고 있다

천년 묵은 느티나무 뿌리도
강풍에 멍이 들어
실바람 소리를 낸다

해송이 파도 음으로 연주를 하면
가파른 산속의 수목들은
휘파람 소리로 합창을 한다
민초에 묻혀 사는 들풀까지도
덩달아 춤을 춘다
입술을 비죽이는
바람 소리로

Wind

My heart trembles
It is stuffy with no vacancy
But wind penetrates deeply
It stirs the heart with soft waves

A thousands of year old beech
Shocked by the strong wind
It makes faint sound like a breeze

Beach pines play the sea waves
Trees on the hills
Hails in full choir
Wild grasses dance together
Along with the wind
Twisting lips with the wind.

낙엽 길

사색(思索)으로 얼룩진 낙엽 길엔
가냘픈 코스모스 춤사위를 펴고
구절초 방긋 방긋 손짓을 하면

굽이쳐 흐르던 계곡은
어느덧 스산한 물줄기를 내 품고
사랑 노래 구슬피 울어 댄다

세월은 가면무도회처럼
오색찬란한 여운을 입고
꿈과 낭만은 지루한 침묵으로
해거름을 밟고 있다

서녘의 빛이 돌고 돌아
또 다른 상념을 꽃피울 때면
인고(忍苦)의 시간은 저 만치 비켜서서
푸른 꿈을 향한 축복의 잔을 들고 있다

내면의 충돌이 무지개로 피어올라
색색이 아롱지는 추억을 찾아
갈잎 한 장 날려 보낸다

The Road of Fallen Leaves

Meditation occupies the road of fallen leaves
Cosmoses toss their heads and dance
Hosts of Siberian chrysanthemums gesticulate

The running valley water
Changes its stream into gloom
It sings sadly the love song

Time is like a masked ball
Reverberation shines brilliantly
In various colors
Dream and romance tread
Silently the sunset

Twilight of the west sky
Bloom other meditation
The time of patient endurance
Glasses of blessing for blue dream

A inside collision becomes a rainbow
An oak leave will be flown
Searching for colorful reminiscence.

굴렁쇠 인생

빠르게 느리게
굽이굽이 고개 넘어
아흔 아홉 굴렁쇠 인생

높고 푸르게
넓고도 아름답게
버리지 못한 자존만을 지키며
고행의 길 살아 온 삶

호롱불 기둥삼아
쌓아온 공든 탑
찬 서리 모진 풍파
누가 알리요

세월 지나 눈을 뜨니
흰 구름 한 점 허공만 날고 있네

Life would Be a Hoop

Hurriedly and slowly
Cross over ridges at every bend
My life is like ninety nine hoops

High and blue
Broad and beautiful
I have kept self-respect
Which I did not lose
I have been living the way of penance

All day and night
I have built an elaborate tower
Cold frost and atrocious wind and waves
Who does know it?

Time and tide have passed
I awoke to find
That a cloud floats in the empty sky.

나 홀로 남으리

찬란한 빛 찾아
모여든 생명체들

푸른빛 잃어가 붉게 물드니
산새도 풀벌레도
하나 둘 떠나고

무리 짓는 들짐승
줄지어 떠나간다

철따라 빛 따라 변신의 마술사는
황홀의 날개 달고 배회하지만
푸른빛 지고나면 어디로 갈까

잃어간 푸른빛 가꾸어가는
밝은 지혜 가진 자 묵묵히 앉아
초롱불 밝혀가며 꿈을 낚는다

I Will Be Alone

Living things get together
In search for brilliant lights

Green changes to red
Mountain birds and grass worms
They leave one by one

Throngs of wild animals
Also leave herd by herd

Every season and every light
Magicians disguise and wander with wings
Where do they go after green disappears?

A sage cherishes green color
He sits silently by lamplight
And he angles for dreams.

그림자(1)

누군가 내 곁을 동행 한다
불러도 대답 없는
그러나 분명 흔적을 따라 함께 한다

한 생을 내 곁에 머물며
꽃비가 되고
꽃눈 되어
슬픈 기린의 목으로 살아 온 너

음지(陰地) 보다 양지(陽地)만을
선호한 넌
진정 내 친구 내 분신이다

An Shadow(1)

Someone goes together with me
There is no answer to my calling
But there is an evident trace

Through life you have stayed beside me
You are compared with
The flowers of rain and snow
You have lived with
A sorrowful neck of a giraffe

You like better a sunny place
Than a shady place
Really you are the other self of a friend.

그림자(2)

불러도 대답이 없는 사람
손짓 발짓 쌍둥이로만 다가선 너

생을 바쳐 지키느라
고생도 많았을 터
고맙고 안타까움에
목메어 떨리는 구나

사시사철
꽃비 되고 꽃눈 되어
주군을 지키던 넌

참으로 가련한 양지의 사나이구나

An Shadow(2)

You does not answer to my calling
You are accompanied by me
As a twin moving hands and feet

Through life you keep companionship
In spite of privation and severity
I greatly appreciate the situation
I am suffocated by impatience

Through all the four seasons
You take care of me
As if I am an emperor

Indeed you are a sympathetic
Man in a sunny place.

첩첩이 쌓인 일상의 풍광
이미 일차원이 아닌
삼차원의 세계에서
겹으로 덧칠해진
삶의 굴레

The scenes are heaped with routines
Already it is not one dimension
But three dimensions
The bridle of life
Has been painted twofold

제3부

하얀 마음

The White Heart

함께 가는 길

꿈과 낭만
환희의 꽃동산에
한그루 동백(冬柏) 심어두고
둘이서 하나 되어
정성껏 꽃 피우던 날

삼복더위
혹한의 추위에도
고갤 떨구고
축복의 미소로 열매 맺는다

떡잎의 푸른 숲
짙은 윤기 발하여
희년(禧年)의 세월위에
깃발로 달려온 인생

무거운 껍질 속
하얀 미소의
겨울 꽃으로 피어난다

Going along One Way Together

Dream and romance
In the flower hill of delight
We planted a camellia
Two became one
The bloomed day of sincerity

In the midsummer heat
In the midwinter cold
It drops the head and bears fruit
With the smile of congratulations

Green woods of cotyledons
With dense gloss
In the long time
With a flag the life has dashed

In a heavy bark
With a white smile
The flower of winter blooms.

이율배반

사랑과 미움은
항상 두 점을 오가는 선상에서
서로가 서로를 밀고 당기며
반쪽의 정을 묻고 존재한다

그러던 어느 날
서로가 등 돌려
이율배반이 창 너머 바람으로
서성이다가 돌아선다면

사랑도 미움도
모두 다 날려 보내
다시 찾지 않으리

그래도 못 잊는 그리움 하나
꿈길을 맴돌 때면
총총 걸음으로 달려가
가슴에 묻어놓고

미움 너머로 보낸 사랑
사랑 너머로 보낸 그대
또 다른 사랑으로 꽃 피우리

Antinomy

Love and hatred
On the line coming and going always
Between two points
Pushing and pulling each other
There is burying for half of affection

Then one day
Turn the back to each other
Antinomy winds down the window
If you would linger and turn

Even love and hatred
Send everything to blow
Never found again

You also can not forget the one longing
When you spin round dreaming road
Running in quick short steps
Buried in the heart

Love sent over hatred
You sent over love
Blossom by another flower of love.

가을 엽서

싸늘함이 있습니다
뼈를 앗아깍는 아픔으로
붉은 물결은
뚝뚝 떨어지고 있습니다
내가 사랑하는 모든 것들이
칼바람에 스쳐
허공을 맴돌고
슬픔은 가슴 밑바닥에 깔려
흐느끼고만 있습니다
저리 붉고 고운
황금빛 갈잎 엽서가
귓가에 달려들어
은밀한 사랑을 속삭입니다
그가 가고 없는
공허의 터에
내가 있음을 일깨우고
가로등 밑을 따라
옷깃을 여미는 둘 만의
발길을 재촉합니다

The Postcard of Autumn

It is rather chilly
Painfully to the bone
Red waves drop water
All things that I love turn around
The empty sky owing to cold wind
Sorrow sobs at the bottom of heart
That red and pretty postcard
It a golden fallen leal
Which whispers secret love
To my ears
It went away
I am at a void site
Along the street light
We two are awestruck
We two gurry our way.

갈매기

산 좋고 물 좋은
반도(半島)의 인심(人心)속에
묻혀 살다가
어느 때인가 빛바랜
저 하늘이 싫어져서
그냥 그렇게 떠나온 거야

보고 싶지 않고
듣고 싶지 않으며
말하고 싶지 않은 도시를 떠나
나 홀로 예까지 찾아온 거야

바람 따라 출렁이는 파도에 쓸려
멍든 가슴 조용히 녹이고 싶어
날개 접고 먼 길 떠나온 거야

싱그러운 바다 내음
코끝에 묻고
한 세상 조용히 살고 싶은 거야

A Sea gull

I lived in a peninsula
Where beautiful mountains
And clear rivers were
And also good-hearted people were
Once I became averse to the dull sky
I left there and came here

Neither anything I wish to look at
Nor listen to, nor speak to
I left there and came here alone

I came here from afar
Along the wind and waves
And I fold my wings
To heal quietly my bruised heart

I wish to live my whole life
Here quietly
Breathing the fresh sea smell.

축제의 날

젊음이
광란의 몸부림으로
불타오를 땐
진한 추억의 샘물
넘쳐흐른다
세상은 온통
사랑의 빛으로 물들여 있고
파도에 쓸린 세월은
그리움의 무게를 안고
진실을 토해내는 해후가 된다
마지막 축제의 불꽃놀이
여인의 발렌타인

Festival Day

When youth flames out
With crazy swinging
The fountain water overflows
With distinct reminiscence
Never does the world more ardently
Steep in such lovely splendour
Time sweeps with currents
Bearing the weight of yearning
Time becomes an encounter
Which vomits truth
The last fireworks of the festival
Valentine of a woman.

친구야

세월의 뒤안길에
흰 서리 내리고
깊게 파인 주름살
생(生)을 노래한다

바람처럼 스쳐간
그 젊음 그 정열
꿈은 날아가고
추억만 남았구나

친구야
영글지 못한 깊은 우정
남은 세월에 담아서
허허로운 웃음으로
깊은 정(情) 나눠 갖자

To a Friend

Behind time and change
Your hairs are white like frost
The deep wrinkles sing your career

Youth and passion have gone
Like the wind
Dreams have flown away
And remimiscences have left

My bosom friend
Soak in the remaining time
The unripe friendship
Let us share it kindly
Out of the rearing laughter.

하얀 마음

설원의 풍광으로 시작되는
새해의 아침
맑고 깨끗한 하얀 마음으로 살련다

가슴 뛰는 첫사랑의 순정처럼
청순한 하얀 마음으로

굳게 마음먹은 새 출발의 각오
강한 의지와 변치 않은 하얀 마음

불의에 굴하지 않은 정의처럼
올곧은 사상의 하얀 마음으로

처음과 끝이 하나인
일관된 정신의 하얀 마음

오늘도 내일도
일생을 그렇게
희고 흰
하얀 마음으로 살련다

The White Heart

New Year's morning
Begins with a sonw field
I wish to live
With a serene and white heart

With a clean and white heart
Like the passion of first love

The new start of the year with strong will
With unchangeable white heart

Unflinching to unrighteousness
Right-minded thought and white heart

From the beginning to the end
Consistent mind and white heart

Today and even tomorrow
I live all my life
With that so white heart.

유년의 추억
— 회상

그리도 추운 11살의 겨울
어머니의 품속을 떠난
어스름 해질녘이면
초롱한 눈망울에 이슬 맺힌
흐느낌
몸 무개보다 더한 책가방 메고
밤길 걸어 찾은 할머니의 품속

꿈속에서도 솟구쳐 오른
어머니의 그리움
해맑은 동생들의 눈동자
꿈에서 깨어나
훌쩍이는 눈물 닦아주며 들려주신
한석봉의 이야기는
할머니의 단골 메뉴였다

이제 그 자리에 선 난
아무에게도 들려줄 이야기가 없다

Recollections of Childhood
— Reminiscence

In a very cold winter day
When I was eleven years old
I left home and mother
I went to school at grandmother's home
At sunset I used to weep
I carried heavy book bag with me
The bag was as much heavy as my weight

In a dream I yearned mother
I thought of the clean eyes of
My young brothers and sisters
Grandmother wiped out my tears
She used to tell me Han Seok-Bong tale

Now I am grandfather
But I don't have tales
To tell anybody.

허무(虛無)(2)

기나긴
인생(人生) 역정
무한대의 변화 속에

가고 싶어 갔고
오고 싶어 왔으며
놀고 싶어 놀고
먹고 싶어 먹었으며

내 하고픈 모든 것
다 해 보았으나

남는 건 오직
빈주먹 공간뿐

성공도 실패도
마지막 순간엔
허무와 허탈의
참회 일뿐

Nihility(2)

Through the past journey of life
In the innumerable changes

I went because I wanted to go
I came because I wanted to come
I played because I wanted to play
I ate because I wanted to eat

I have done
All that I wanted to do

But what remains
Is only an empty fist

At the last moment
Success and failure
Are the only contrition
Of nihility and emptiness.

적막

내 가졌던 화려한 날개
수명을 다하니

하늘을 날아도
산을 올라도
기류를 잡지 못하고

불같이 뿜어대던
벨소리마저 졸음을 좇고 있다

뜬눈으로 지샌 지난날의 세월들
여가(餘暇)의 낭만을 꿈꾸었는데
하루가 무섭게
적막이 감돈다

내 가진 소망과 보람 어디가고
회상의 깃털만 날리며
꾸벅꾸벅 시간을 잠재우고 있다

Loneliness

My luxurious wings have expired

Both flying in the sky
And mountain climbing
Cant not catch the current of air

Even the loud sound of telephone
Seems to be sleepy

In the sleepless old days
I dreamed leisure and romanticism
Now everyday loneliness turns round

My long cherished wish and benefit
Where have they gone
The feather of recollection files
I idly let time sleep.

욕망

인간은 누구나 욕망의 꿈을 꾸며 살아간다

욕망이란 순수를 지향하는 정의 일 땐 화려하나
순수를 저버릴 땐 욕심과 야욕으로 물들여
패망의 원인이기도 하다

순수와 진실,
소망과 인내의 숲
지혜와 용기가
욕망의 근원이라면

부와 권력을 향한 집념과 야욕
명예와 허영을 위한 노력은
악의 축이며 패망의 길이듯

순수와 진실을 위한
지혜의 욕망을 꿈꾸는 것이
인간의 도리인 것을

Desire

Man lives dreaming desire

Desire is gorgeous when it is justice
That points to purity
But without purity and desire is nothing but cupidity
Then it could become the reason of ruin

If purity and genuineness
The forests of wish and perseverance
Wisdom and courage
Those were the origin of desire

Tenacity and cupidity pointing to richness and power
Endeavor for honor and vanity
Might be the axis of evil and lead ruin

For purity and genuineness
To foster wisdom and desire
Should be the duty of man.

초암산 철쭉꽃

남도의 끝자락에 선
작고도 아담한
운무에 쌓인 초암산의 능선
신록의 푸르름이 오기 전
온통 불의 바다를 이룬 철쭉꽃의 환희여!

바위틈 사이사이 마다
울긋불긋 삼보향(三寶鄕)을 세기고
조국독립의 원혼이 깃든 고장

북향하는 보성강 줄기에
엉겅퀴, 노린재꽃 야생화로 자라
오월의 축제에 빛을 더하는 구나

A Royal Azalea Blossom of Mt. Choam

Standing on the edge of the South Province
Too small, compact
The ridge of Mt. Choam veiled in cloud and mist
Before coming verdant greenery
The delights of royal azalea blossom
Accomplished of the sea of fire!

Between the every crevices of rocks
Carving bright-colored Sambo-Province
Province infused with the furies
Of the independent fatherland

The course of Bosung River to northward
Thistle, stinkbug-flower grow as wild flowers
Adding the light on the festival of May.

공간의 미학

삶이 허공을 돌아
생각과 말과 행동으로 맺어질 때
공간은 언제나 가득 채워지는 것

마음도 물질도
필요한 자에게 주어 나를 비우면
또 다른 상념이 그득해 지는 여유의 장(場)

좋은 것 귀중한 것
골라서 주고나면
행복도 보람도 두 배로 쌓이는 부(富)의 방(房)

말과 글은 더욱 더 그러하니
아낌없이 주고서
풍요롭게 가꾸어
풍성한 삶의 근원이 되었으면

마음의 공간은 비운만큼 채워지는
옹달샘과 같은 것
비워도 비워도 가득 채워진
공간의 미학이여

The Aesthetics of Space

Life turns around the air
When it is joined in thought, word, and action
The space will be filled at any time

Heart and substance
Emptying me given to whom needs them
Another conception of a space that is filled with
leisure

After picking and giving the good and valuables
Happiness and reward
Accumulate double in the wealthy room

What is spoken and written
Will give more generously
And grow plentifully
It might be the source of abundant life

Clearing of the mind as much as the space is
filled
Like a small spring
Empty and empty but fulfilling
The aesthetics of the space.

바람처럼 스쳐간
그 젊음 그 정열
꿈은 날아가고
추억만 남았구나

Youth and passion have gone
Like the wind
Dreams have flown away
And remimiscences have left

제4부

숲속의 대화

Dialogue in the Forest

숲속의 대화

굽이쳐 올라가는 계룡산 기슭엔
칠순 노파와 가족을 이룬
산새들, 산짐승들
이심전심 가슴이 통한
나무와 돌들의 대화

백설이 뒤덮인 첩첩 산중에
먹이를 나르는 노파의 정성은
깃털의 심장과 포효한 동물들의
가슴을 녹여주는 깊은 향수

새벽의 미소가 그들을 깨우면
어제의 안녕과 내일을 축복하는
눈빛, 목소리
골짜기에 흐르는 해맑은 옥구슬 소리는
따끈한 녹차의 향기

마주치지 못하는 하루의 시작은
불안과 초조로 흐느끼고 울부짖는
그들만의 대화
사랑의 여운이다

Dialogue in the Forest

At the foot of steep Mt Geryong
A seventy-year-old woman lives
With mountain birds and beasts
Communicant by heart
The dialogue between trees and stones

Snow-clad mountain valley
The old woman carries feed gladly
She calms the beasts' howling
And warms their hearts

The smile at dawn wakes them up
There are the glitter of eyes and voice blessing
Yesterday and tomorrow
The sounds of flowing waters in the valley
Are the fragrance of green tea

When they don't all meet together
The day begins with unrest and stir
And cries and howls
It is their own dialogue
It is also the reverberation of love.

일출

까맣게 드리운 잿빛 먹구름
하늘을 덮고 땅을 덮고
내 마음까지 뒤덮어
무거운 침묵으로 짓눌린 새벽녘

홍조 띤 햇살은
붉은 가슴 드러내고
저 바다 저 하늘 끝자락에 서서
환호의 탄성으로 솟아오른다

한 풀 한 풀 벗겨지는
무거운 침묵
희망과 사랑으로
빛을 밝히니
화려한 날개로 비상하리라

The Sunrise

Gray clouds that hang down blackly
Spread over the sky and land
Besides my mind
In the dawn that weighed down
With the burden of silence

Flushed sunshine
Bares it's reddened the breast
Stands on the edge of the sea and the sky
And rises with shouting of joy

Slipping off one by one
The burden of silence
With hope and love
Brightened light
Soar with brilliant wings.

더 좋은 사람

코발트 빛 눈동자
해맑은 미소
넘치는 위트로
따뜻한 가슴 열어주는
마음편한 사람

그대를 만나는 순간은
장미 빛 꽃술입니다

해묵은 관념에
상상의 날개 달아주며
흐트러진 몸매에
정렬된 담백함으로
새둥지 만들어 준 사람

그대와 함께 할수록
더 좋은 사람
영원한 꿈길입니다

A Better Person

Your eyes are the color of cobalt
With bright smile and overflowing wits
You open your warm heart
You are a comfortable person

The moment I met you
You are a rosy pistil

To an old concept
You bind the wings of imagination
I was disturbed
But you made me in good order
You also made me a new nest

Because you are with me
You are a better person
It is an eternal way of dream.

작은 가슴 큰 사랑

아침 마다
띵동
작은 사랑이 온다

꼬막죽 작은 손엔
올망졸망

정(情)도
마음(心)도
사랑(愛)도
가득 가득 들려있다

목발 짚는 친구의
멍에를 지고
오손도손 나누는
큰 빛 사랑이여

작은 가슴
큰 사랑
영원하여라

Little Heart and Great Love

Every morning
Ding-dong
Little love come

Small hands holds ark shell porridge
In a lovely ruddle

Sentiment
Heart
Love
All are fully carries about

A friend walks on crutches
Put the yoke of love or oneself
Talks intimately
Love of great light

Little heart
Great love
Be eternal.

마음의 바다

잔잔한 가슴에 먹구름 드리워
진한 파도가 치면
간밤에 깃을 세우고 떠난
갈매기의 끼룩거리는 소리가
귓전을 때린다

은빛 모래위에 창을 매달고
토해내는 해후는
당신의 여운일까
돌아서는 그림자 일까

내 마음의 바다는
지금도 하이 얀 조가비의 꿈 되어
두둥실 밀려오는 해조음으로
당신의 심장을 고동치게 하련만

빛바랜 가슴의 열기
다시 불러 모아
칠월의 태양으로 불꽃을 피우련다

The Sea of Heart

The clouds in my calm heart
The sea waves wildly
I can hear sea gull cry
The bird ruffled up its feathers
When it left here last night

Through the window in the silvery sand
Vomiting encounter might
Be your reverberation
Or your turning shadow

The sea of my heart
Even now it becomes
The dream of white shells
The casting sound of the sea
Would beat your heart

I will call again the decolored
Passion of the heart and it flames
With the sun of July.

하늘재

조령산 줄기타고 나지막이 자리한 곳
중원의 꿈 저버린
마이태자 통한의 눈물이
미륵사 계곡을 굽이돌고
포함산 허리엔
고승의 목탁소리 간데없고
솔바람 소리만
옥개석에 잠들어 있다

제국의 경계를 넘나든
천년의 영화는
안개 속에 뒤덮여
주름진 세월만 물들이고
그 옛날의 전설만 되새기는
하늘재 바람

Haneuljae

Along the Mt. Joryeong
In the low-place
Prince Mai who abandoned Jungwon dream
His tears flow around
The valley Mireuk Temple
At the foot Mt. Poham
Prelate's sound of a wood block
Has gone and the wind of
Pine trees blows

The prosperity of Kingdom of thousand
Years are fogged
Wrinkled time and the old legend
Are in the Haneuljae wind.

행복의 미학

소유와 힘의 논리가
작은 기쁨 줄 수 있으나
가슴을 뜨겁게 지필 수 는 없는 것

떡잎에 흔들리는 푸르름처럼
빛과 사랑
꽃과 인연
물과 베풂의 연분이
훈훈한 정으로 모아져
마음속에 흐르는 행복이어라

나눔과 봉사
깊이 있는 사색의 강(江)이
유한 심리로 도도히 흐를 때
청정한 하늘빛 가슴이 열리어
신(神)의 소리로 웃을 때
비로소 느껴지는 환한 깨우침
거기에
그것이 있다

The Aesthetics of the Happiness

The logic of possession and power
Although it can give a little joy
Can't make fire heart hot

Like budding greenery swaying in
Light and love
Flower and affinity
Predestination of water and benefaction
gathered in heart-warming feelings
Flowing happiness in the hearts!

Sharing and service
When the river of deep contemplation
Stream of profluent mentality flow down
Open the heart that pure azure
When laugh out sound of god
Finally enlightened felt brightly
There
There it is.

마음의 향기

아름답다
님 향한
마음의 발길

성스럽다
무릎 꿇고 두 손 모아
기도하는 마음

거룩하다
참회의 눈물 쏟으며
고백하는 마음

영원하여라
참 빛 발하는
용해된 마음이여

The Fragrance of Heart

It is beautiful
The steps of heart to you

It is sacred
Kneel and get together two hands
The praying heart

It is holy
To shed penitential tears
The heart of confession

Be eternal
To illuminate real light
The heart of resolution.

등대

칠흑 같은 밤하늘
별자리 헤이며
출렁이는 모터소리
하이얀 파도여

저 만치 비켜선
깜박등 불빛은
북두칠성 자리매김
오가는 뱃머리 길을 터준다

망망대해(大海) 침묵 속에
컨테이너 철선(鐵船)은
이국항(異國港) 불 밝히며
뱃고동 울어 댄다

낮과 밤을 헤이는
파도 넘어 이국땅
낙조의 여울 따라
등불 밝혀 꿈길 열어준다

A Lighthouse

I count the constellation
In the night sky pitch-black
Rolling sound of motors
White waves!

Flickering light stands alone
As much as that
And it opens the way for
The Great Bear and the bow to come and go

Container wire
In a silence of a vast expanse of water
Lights a foreign country
And a boat whistle cries out

A foreign country beyond waves
Comes along with rapids of the setting sun
A lighthouse is operating a day and night
Lights and it opens dream way.

만남이 좋은 사람

밝은 미소와 예의 바른 자세로
배려와 양보로 사랑과 믿음 주는
온화한 사람

독서와 사색으로
풍요로운 지혜와 철학이 있어
신뢰와 비전을 주는 사람

작은 일에도 감사하며
균형 잡힌 사고로 확신에 찬 미래를 논하며
성공을 예단하는 사람

겸손과 감사로
따뜻한 가슴 열어 세상을 치유하는
그런 사람 아닐까

Good Man to Meet

With bright smile and courteous posture
With solicitude and concession
Gives love and belief
Moderate man

With reading and meditation
With abundant wisdom and philosophy
Man who gives faith and vision

Appreciate trivial matters
Balanced thinking discusses
The confident future
Man who predicts success

With humility and thanks
Open heartedly and warmly heals the world
Such man would be good man.

희망봉

'아메리칸 드림'의 꿈을 안고
하늘 저 편 바다 건너 온 땅
미지의 넓은 대륙에
꿈과 희망 가꾸어 온지
어언 100년

언어도, 문화도,
인종도 다른 이 땅에
풍요로운 밭을 가꾸어온
자랑스런 이 민족
동방의 햇볕이여,

그대들의 드높은 꿈
저 자유의 여신상에 걸어두고
밤과 낮
해와 별을 바라보며
용솟음치는 기개(氣槪)로
탑을 쌓아
희망의 나라, 민족의 나라
합창하여라

그대들 있기에
광활한 대지에 금광이 맥을 잇고

The Torch of Hope

With the 'American dream'
You crossed over the Pacific Ocean
One hundred years have already passed
Since you have raised the dream and hope
In this vast unknown American Continent

In the land of different language
Different culture and race
You have cultivated a fertile field
You are the proud Korea people
The sunlight of the Orient

The lofty dream of yours
You have hung it up to The Statue of Liberty
Day and night looking up at the sun and stars
You have erected a high tower
With spouting spirit
Sing in chorus all together
The land of hope and democracy

You exist to join in
Continuing to cultivate the vein of gold
On this spacious earth

푸르른 생명의 원천은 끝이 없도다
아, 자랑스런 동방의 거인들이여
민족의 등불이여,
인류의 희망이여

The source of green life is endless
Ah! proud giant of the Orient
You are the torch of our nation
You are the hope of humankind.

문향의 고장

태백산 계곡 따라 굽이굽이 흐르다
목계장터 뗏목에 어린 술 추념의 신경림
화암리 수문위엔 권오순의 보슬비
슬픔으로 가슴 매운 비목의 한명회는
시인의 탯줄로 자리 잡은
반도의 중원
충주의 기상인가

하늘과 땅과 사람이 모인
천등 지등 인등의
세 여울은
삼탄의 한 얼굴

남한강 달천강
탄금성 휘도는
격전의 배수지엔
탄천대에 한(恨)을 묻는
신립장군 원혼은
가야금 줄에 울고만 있다

The Place of Literary Fragrance

River flows along
The Mts. Taeback valley
At Mokge market bar
Poet Shin Kyung-Lim drinks
On the sluice gate at Hwaam-ri
Kwon Oh-Soon's drizzling rain
Han Myung-Hoi's sad heart
The site of poets' navel cords
The middle of Korea Peninsula
Literary temper of Choongju

Sky, Earth and Man stand for
Three rivers: Cheondeung, Jideung, and Indeung
Those are the faces of Samtan

The Dalcheon River of the South Han River
Tangeumsung of a hard-fought field
Taken up with a river
Behind the troops
General Shinlip with the grudge
of Tancheondae
His soul is weeping
Along with the strings of a gayageum.

코발트 빛 눈동자
해맑은 미소 넘치는 위트로
따뜻한 가슴 열어주는
마음편한 사람
그대를 만나는 순간은
장미 빛 꽃술입니다

Your eyes are the color of cobalt
With bright smile and overflowing wits
You open your warm heart
You are a comfortable person
The moment I met you
You are a rosy pistil

제5부

광야

The Open Field

광야

태양의 열기로 타오르는
푸르른 광야
쏟아지는 역동의 힘으로
빛을 발하여
새천년의 두 해가 밝았도다

소리 높여 외쳐라
땅이 꺼져 지진이 일어나듯
묵은 때 훨훨 벗어
광란의 빛으로 떠올라
청기어린 굳은 팔 번쩍들어라

용솟음치는 가슴들
활짝 열고
저 하늘이 붉도록
늘푸른 광야에 씨를 뿌려
새벽이슬로 꽃피우리니

빛나거라, 영광되라
찬란한 역사 앞에

The Open Field

The sun glows
Above the open green field
With the light of dynamic power
Two years of the New Millennium
Have already passed

Hail aloud
As if volcanoes break out
Dust off
Float with the light of fervour
Lift sturdy arms

Open the leaping hearts
To make the sky red
Sow seeds in the evergreen field
They bloom with dawn dew

Be bright, be glorious
Before the brilliant history

아!
사랑하는
나의 태양
나의 조국
나의 형제여

Oh! Beloved
My Sun
My Country
My Brethren.

역사의 꽃
— 문화의 열매

외로움의 목소리가
서녘 한 줄기 빛
보리피리로 들어와
가냘픈 희망의 날개 펄럭인다

고목들의 가지에는 꽃 피우지 못한 채
어린 실가지에 매달린 화려한 송이
역사의 찬란함을 잉태한다

힘 있는 자, 가진 자의 목소리는
허공을 맴돌지만
문화마당 일구려는 뜨거운 울림
민초의 열매로 주렁주렁 열리니

장하다 그 이름
빛난다 그 얼굴
내 그대위해
영원토록 꽃 피우리니
영원토록 짙은 향 뿜으리니

The Flower of History
— The Fruit of Culture

The voice of loneliness
Like a slant of light of the west
Flickers soft wings of hope
As a barley pipe

Upon branches of an aged tree
Flowers didn't bloom
Upon twigs of a young tree
Beautiful flowers pollinate
Brilliant history

Powerful and rich people's voice is void
Hot echo establishes culture yard
The fruit of common people is abundant

The name is great
The face is bright
I make flowers bloom
I make fragrance be forever for you.

월출산(月出山)

남도의 소금강
영산강 젖줄기 끼고
굽이굽이 깎아지른
기암괴석 사이사이로
정절의 노송들이
하이얀 발톱을 들어내어
억만년의 무궁함을 자랑하는
천왕봉, 국사봉, 구정봉이여

중첩된 산줄기 따라 펼쳐지는
장엄하고 찬란한 일출(日出)
다도해 바라보며 서해로 떨어지는
붉게 채색된 일몰(日沒)
주지봉 위로 솟구쳐 오른 월출(月出)은
하늘이 내려준 천혜의 장엄함을
어이타 잊고 있나

바람이 스쳐 휘감기는
억새들의 춤추는 모습은
굽힐 줄 모르는 정절의 고향임을 노래하는
월출산의 기상이여

Mt. Wolchul Moonrise

The Sokeum River of the Southern province
Along the Youngsan River breast
Among the rocks and stones
Of meandering cliffs
Time-honoured pine trees
Explode white paws
Make a boast of constancy
For billions of years
Cheonwangbong, Guksabong, and Gujeongbong.

The sublime and brilliant sunrise
Spreads over overlapped mountains
The red sunset
To the west facing thr East Sea
How could the moonrise over the Jujibong
Forget its heaven-born grandeur?

Dancing reed in the wind
The spirit of Mt. Wolchul Moonrise
Singing the place of honesty
Across the continent

대륙을 넘어 히말라야의 정상까지
그 기개(氣槪)를 드높이 떨쳐
세세만년(世世萬年) 향내 띄워
영원무궁(永遠無窮) 꽃피워라

Up to the summit of the Himalayas
With the spirit and eternal frangrance
Blooming forever and ever.

눈꽃 축제

잿빛 하늘에 나부끼는
하이얀 점박이들의 축제
뽀송한 따스함이 가슴을 여밀 때면
저 만치 다가서는 추억의 노래

재롱이도 다롱이도
허공을 향한
포효의 노래 부를 때면
무릎을 감싸는 폭설의 잔치

아득히 잊혀진 사랑의 맹세
찬란했던 그 시절 떠나버리고
마른 가지 풀섶으로 뒹구는
짧은 환희의 순간들

이제 함박꽃 눈송이 되어
청춘을 노래하고
해맑은 세상 얼음 꽃으로 피워
눈부신 청춘 다시 한 번 살자꾸나

Snow-white Festival

Snow drifts against the grey sky
A festival of white dots
My heart thaws and warms
Songs of remembrance are heard closer

Even Jerongee and Daerongee
Are singing to the snowing sky
Snow is heaped to the knees
The feast of heavy snow

The forgotten vow of first love
Gone are the glorious days
Bare twigs are dry
Short moments of rapture

I sing of past youth
Seeing the snowflakes like flower leaves
Ice flowers make the world purer
I return to dazzling youth again.

가을

화려한 단풍으로 반사되어 버린
노을 빛
하얀 조개구름 붉게 물들이고
날개 접고 비행하는
꿈속의 여행

휘늘어진 감나무엔
소담스런 추억들이 주렁주렁 매달려
붉게 익어가고
옷깃을 스치는 고뇌(苦惱)는
바람의 무게만큼
깊어만 간다

Autumn

Splendidly scarlet-tinged leaves
Reflected sunset is today's color
The sunset has dyed white cirrocumulus
Furl the wings and fly
Journey in a dream

Pleasant recollections are in full bearing
On the drooped down persimmon trees
They are ripening red
An affliction that goes past by the collars
Is deepening as much as the weight of wind.

삶 터

오천여 생명의 연줄
힘찬 발돋움에
찬란한 역사 이룬
우리의 삶 터

휘두른 칼날에
분해된 영혼 되어
조각조각 흩어져
눈물 흘릴 때
쓰라린 상처는
지울 길 없네

어이하여
이 아픔 어루만져서
재기(再起)의 삶터를
가꾸어 볼까

The Site of Living

Over five thousand people live
With a dynamic tiptoe
Our site of living
Has achieved a brilliant history

By a brandished blade
Becomes a piecemeal soul
And disperses into little pieces
Like shed tears
Afflicted bruises
Can not be cleansed

How to stroke the sore
How to cultivate
Living site of restoration.

인생의 꽃
— 황혼의 들녘에 핀 꽃

세월의 중량으로 농익은 삶의 지혜
몸과 마음이 따로이던 젊은 시절
욕망과 절정 묻어두고
외길로만 살아온 인생길

지난날
잠재웠던 활화산 같은 시혼(詩魂)에
푸르른 꿈을 키워
황혼의 들녘에 서서
문학의 씨앗 가꾸어간
님이시여

실버들의 천국에
주름진 계곡마다 굽이굽이 흐르는
소담스런 하얀 이야기 꽃
주저리 주저리 엮어
만개하고픈 꿈동산이여

장하오이다
영광스럽소이다
문학의 갈증 꽃피우려는
백설의 청춘이여

The Flower of Life
— A Flower in the Twilight Field

The ripen wisdom of life
Along with the weight of life
When young body was apart from spirit
And desire was put aside
You have lived along one way

In the passed days the spirit of poetry slept
But it is like an active volcano
Blue dream has grown
At the sunset you write poems

In the Heaven of slender willow
At each valley white flowers of tales
Look nice and ripe
It's a hill of the dream
That is to bloom fully
On the hill of dreams

You are great and honorable
You intend to bloom literature
You are a youth of snow

인생의 구석구석 삶의 지혜 엮어내어
오늘의 영광 글꽃을 피우오니
후세만민(後世萬民)에 커다란 빛이 오이다
장엄한 영광의 축제이오이다

길이 영광 누리소서
길이 축복 누리소서

You organize the wisdom of life
And bloom the flower of glory
It will become big light
For the people of next generations
It is a magnificent festival of glory

May your days be glorious
May your days be blessed.

하나 되는 세계로
— 축제의 꽃

동방의 작은 빛
온 인류와 유성들 밝히나니
태양도 눈부셔 횡성을 앞세우고
찬연한 빛 찾아 마음을 적신다

인류의 평화와 사랑과 나눔의 축제
반도에서 성화를 밝히나니
자랑스런 영광이여
뜻깊은 제전이라

칠천만 민족 하나 되는 마음으로
그대들 반기오니
앞서거라 뒤서거라
어서들 오소서

우리 모두 손에 손잡고 발에 발 묶어
사랑과 평화 누리면서
성전에 불사른 오륜의 축제
태양이 무섭도록 밝은 빛 쏟아 내어
하나 되는 인류 건설 만들어 가자

Toward One World
— The Flower of Festival

Small light of the Far East
Illuminates all mankinds and planets
The sun dazzles with brilliant light
The hearts become wet

The festival is for the peace and love
In the Korea Peninsula
The Olympic torch burns
It's proud glory
It's a meaningful feast

Seventy million people become one
And welcome world people
Come here ahead or back

We all together hold hand in hand
And share love and peace
The Olympic Game is a holy festival
The sun pours down fearfully bright light
Let us make a legend of one world.

생명

숲은 초록빛 생명으로
삶을 잉태하고
청록색 바람으로
꿈을 가꾸어
빠알간 알몸으로
내일을 찬미한다

Life

Woods bear life
With verdant color
Woods grow dreams
With green wind
Woods praise tomorrow
With naked bodies.

봄이 오는 소리

파아란 숨 내어 쉬며
노오란 미소 띠우더니
연분홍 붉은 함성
봄이 오는 소리

A Sound of Spring Coming

Exhale blue breath
Smile in yellow color
That light pink and red outcry
A sound of spring coming.

서해대교

서쪽 바다 가로지른
기나긴 다리 끝엔
용암으로 녹여 나온
불덩이 하나
유유자적 눈부시다

잔류(殘留)로 출렁이는 일몰의 시간 속에
어둠이 깔려오면
가로등(街路燈) 불빛 따라
상념은 그리움을 불러 세운다

귀로에 나선 갈매기 한 쌍
노을에 적셔
끝없는 방황으로 저공의 날개를 접는다

사랑도 미움도
애틋한 정 쌓았기에
차가운 밤바다 그늘에
무거운 짐 보따리 풀어 놓는다

Grand Bridge of Seohae Sea

Across the West Sea
At the end of the long bridge
A dazzling lump of fire
Formed from molten lava

Under the reverberant twilight
As it grows darker
Thinking calls longing
Along the lighted bridge lamps

A pair of sea gulls going home
Soaks in the setting sun
Folds their wings
After endless wonderings

Love and hatred have gathered
As warm affection
Under the shade of each cold night
Unpack its heavy burden.

민중의 합창

조국 독립과 함께 태동한
민중의 지팡이
어언 70여 성상에 이르렀으니
기쁨도 슬픔도
고난도 역경도
민중 속에 자리한 호돌이와 호순이
장하오이다
고맙소이다

오늘도 민중위한 고난의 시간들
그대 있어 민중(民衆) 있고
민중 있어 그대 있는 세상
우리 함께 어울려 어깨동무 춤을 추자

수원성 푸른 물결
드높은 햇살 아래
정의와 순수의 깃발 휘날리며
민의의 한 마당에
충정의 팡파르 울리자
기상의 나팔 크게 부르자

자랑스런 수원성의 민중이여
자랑스런 수원성의 호돌이여 호순이여

Chorus of People

The National Police was established
As our nation was liberated from Japan
It is more than seventy years old
We call police the stick of people
Police always shares pleasure
Sorrow, and distress with people
Hodori and Hosuni are great
Truly we thank you very much

Everyday police suffers difficulties
People are well owing to you
You exist for nation and people
We all together dance delightedly

Suwon Castle is blue and sunny
We shake the flag of justice and purity
In the plaza of people fanfare sounds

People of proud Suwon Castle
Hodori and Hosuni of proud Suwon Castle.

해설

명상(瞑想)의 숲길

─ 정찬우 시론 ─

최홍규 영문학박사
중앙대 명예교수, 시인, 평론가

정찬우 시인의 제7시집 「달빛에 띄운 연정」을 비롯한 지금까지 발행된 6권의 시집을 영어로 번역하였다. 그 과정에서 그의 시에 대한 독창적인 창의성과 인간애에 담겨진 사랑과 믿음과 그리움과 충성심이란 철학적 사고와 관념을 분석하고 감상하였다. 그러나 한국어 시를 영어로 번역하기는 참으로 어려운 일이다. 두 언어의 문법체계가 전혀 다르기 때문이다.

정 시인의 시에서 중요한 주제는 인간의 사랑과 믿음 그리움과 애환에 대한 심층적 과제를 깊고 넓게 이해하려는 외로운 명상이다. 시에서 섬세하고 합리적 지성의 면모를 미학적 서사와 양식으로 접근하려는 시의 힘이 대단히 강하다. 시가 단순하면서도 명료해서 언어의 통사론적 이해가 매우 높다. 또한 신랄한 재치는 깊은 지성의 자화상이다.

그의 시는 다양한 주제와 형식이 시적 변용을 조화롭게 이루어지도록 직유와 은유 등 비유적 용법을 적절히 사용하고 있다. 그의 시가 고상한 시의 향기와 아름다운 음악성을 지니고 있음이 더욱더 매혹적인 흥미를 북돋운다.

정 시인은 한국 현대문학의 세계화를 위하여 40여년이 넘도록 부단히 노력해 오고 있다. 우리 문학을 외국어로 번역한다는 것은 단순한 언어적 번역만으로 이루어지는 작업이 아니다. 한국인들의 인간애와 정신적 문화적 사상과 철학 까지도 폭넓게 이해 할 수 있도록 하는 작업이다.

따라서 정 시인은 이렇게 번역된 작품들을 외국인들이 쉽게 읽고 이해 할 수 있도록 하기 위하여 영어가 모국어인 원어민인 Edward Richards 박사에게 감수 받았다.

그리하여 이 시집이 해외 대학 도서관과 유명 공공 도서관들에 보내어 지고 있다. 이처럼 정찬우 시인은 한국문학의 세계화 작업에 뒷받침이 되도록 시 창작에 자양분이 되어주고 있다. 독자들은 이 시집에서 적절한 상징성과 시의 힘을 찾을 수 있다. 이 시집은 시를 통하여 인간과 자연, 그리고 역사와 시간과 공간 등을 들여다 볼 수 있는 스펙트럼이다.

정 시인의 지성적 면모와 재능이 시 속에서 가지런히 들어나 보인다. 순수하면서도 역동적인 시 쓰기가 정 시인의 시적 의식과 감수성을 휴머니즘 시인으로 자리매김 하는데 손색이 없다.

Explanation

The Woodland Path of Meditation

— Criticism on Chan-Woo Chung Poetry —

Professor Emeritus of Chung-Ang University in Seoul
translated by Hongkyu A. Choe, Poet, PhD

In the process of the translation of Poet, Chan-Woo Chung's 7th collection of poems whose title is 「*Love in the Moonlight*」. I have analyzed and appreciated the poems. However translation is not easy. Because Korea and English are totally different in the grammar system.

In Chung's poems the understanding of love and human is the main motif. The aesthetic approach and mode are major characteristics. His poems show us exquisite and reasonable mentality with relation to poems. Those poems consist of simplicity and clarity. The trenchant wit is not only deep intelligent self-portait but is common style.

His poems support and nourish promotively the mutiphasic themes of the Korean literature. It is the sign of the poet's intentness he has found a large supply of more complex forms with figurative use of words.

It is with a fascinated interest that one watches the spectacle of the author being so hard on himself for the poems of exaltation and beautiful musicality. The readers of the poems might find not only adequate emblems but also formal worth. This has meant putting the world of human being into parables. The intellectual side of Chung is entirely aligned with most of the poems. The pure kinetic energy of creative writing poems might become an ampler poet consciousness and poetical sensibility. His keen observation results in a scanning of humanism. The strenuousness and the forcing that can be feet in Chung's poems arise from poetically startling spectrum.

Chung poet has steadily made his best endeavors to globalize the contemporary literature of Korea for more than forty years.

To translate literary works is not simple change of syntactic structure. The translation should include Korean human love, cultural and philosophical thoughts so that foreign readers understand enough. The author will donate the books to major university libraries and public libraries of the world. For a perfect translation a linguistic expert, Dr. Edward Richards whose mother tongue is English has helped me in terms of supervision.

시인 약력 : 정찬우 (鄭燦宇)

- 학력
  경희대학교 경영대학 경영학과 졸업
  서울대학교 경영대학원 졸업
  중앙대학교 국제경영대학원 졸업

- 경력
  현우트레이딩(주) 대표이사
  도서출판 밀레 대표이사
  (사)한국수입협회 이사 역임
  (사)한국수입협회 문화예술위원장 역임
  (사)한국수입협회 부회장 역임
  (사)한국수입협회 자문단 의장
  밀레니엄문학회 회장
  (사)세계한민족 책사랑 무궁화 협회 이사장
  살레시안 연합회 부회장
  한국민족문학회 부회장
  (사)한국문인협회 저작권옹호위원
  월간문학편집위원 역임
  (사)한국문인협회 이사 역임
  (사)한국문인협회 감사 역임
  (사)한국문인협회 자문위원
  (사)한국현대시인협회 중앙위원 역임
  (사)한국현대시인협회 이사, 기획위원 역임
  (사)국제펜한국본부 이사, 감사 역임
  (사)국제펜한국본부 자문위원
  KOIMA CEO 합창단 단장
  (사)서울오라토리오 합창단 단원
  (사)난파합창단 단원
  경희동문합창단 단원

About the Author : Chan Woo Chung, Poet

- Education ;
  - BA ; College of Business Administration, Kyunghee University, Seoul
  - MBA ; Graduate School of Business Administration Seoul National University
  - MBA ; Graduate School of International Management Chung Ang University, Seoul

- Experiences ;
  - President of Hyun Woo Trading Co., Ltd.
  - President of the Mille Publishing Cmpany
  - Censor, former Trustee of Korea Importers Association(KOIMA)
  - Director of the Culture and Arts Committee of Korea Importers Association(KOIMA)
  - Forner Vice President of Korea Importers Association(KOIMA)
  - Chaiman of Consultant of Korea Importers Association (KOIMA)
  - Chaiman of the Society of Millennium Literature in Korea
  - Chaiman of the Association of Book love and Hibiscus Syracuse of Korea People in the World
  - Vice President of the Federation of the Korean Salesians
  - Vice President of the Association of Korea National Literature
  - Member of the Copyright Protection Committee of the Korea Writer's Association
  - Member of the Editorial of Monthly Literature Book in Korea Writer's Association
  - Trustee former of Korea Writers Association
  - Censor of Korea Writers Association
  - Consultant Member of Korea Writers Association
  - Central Committee of the Association of Modem Poets in Korea
  - Trustee, Committee of Planning Association of Modem Poets in Korea
  - Former Trustee and Censor of International PEN Korea
  - Consultant member of International PEN Korea Headquarters
  - Director of KOIMA CEO Chorus
  - Members of the Seoul Oratorio Chorus
  - Members of Nanpa Chorus
  - Members of Chrus KyungHee University

- 수상

  부원문학상

  한국민족문학상

  탐미문학상

  문학21문학상

  에피포도문학상(미국)

- 저서

  「다국적 기업의 다국적 마케팅 전력」

  「한국의 플렌트 수출 전략」

- 논문

  「한국기업의 중국투자 진출에 관한 연구」

  「한국의 중남미 전출 전략」 등 다수

- 자서전 대필

  「전쟁과 우정」 정필기

  「생동하는 삶은 역사다」 강두원

- 시집 (한 · 영대역시집)

  「내 영혼의 하얀 미소」

  「내게 사랑 하나 있네」

  「꽃으로 선 당신」

  「가끔은 이런 날이」

  「황홀한 여정」

  「하늘은 내게」

  「달빛에 띄운 연정」

- Literary Prizes ;
  - The Boowon Literature Prize
  - The Korea National Literature Prize
  - Tahmee Literary Prize
  - Literature 21 Prize
  - Epipodo Literary(U.S.A.)

- Books ;
  - Marketing Strategies of Multinations Enterprises
  - The Strategies of Export of Korea, and Others

- Articles ;
  - A Study of Investment in China
  - A Study of Investment in Middle and South Americas

- Biographies Review and slaboration (editorial supervision)
  - War & Friendship
  - The Viatal History of Living

- Korean-English Collection of Poems ;
  - *The Write Smile of my Soul*
  - *There is a Love Me*
  - *You Stand Like A Flower*
  - *Sometimes This Day*
  - *A Fascinating Journey*
  - *The Heaven Is To Me*
  - *Love in the Moonlight*

번역자 약력 : 최홍규 (崔鴻圭)

영문학박사, 시인, 수필가, 문학평론가, 번역가(영어, 불어, 독어)
중앙대학교 영문학과 학사, 서울대학교 영어교육과 석사
동국대학교 영문학과 영문학박사

- 대학 경력
  중앙대학교 인문대학 교수, 명예교수
  미국 하버드대학, 예일대학, 풀브라이트 교환교수
  영국 케임브리지대학, 런던대학(UCL), 객원교수
  프랑스 파리IV대학 (소르본대) 연구교수, 독일 뮌헨대학 초청교수

- 문학관련 경력
  한국문학종교학회장과 한국번역문학회장
  한국농민문학회장, 한국문인협회 문인복지위원
  한국문인협회 한국해외문학 발전위원,
  국제 PEN 한국본부 이사, 자문위원, 국제 PEN 재단 한국대표
  한국시인협회 상임, 중앙위원, 한국문화예술시인연대회장

- 수상
  미국 에피포도 문학상, 국제PEN 번역문학상, 헤밍웨이문학상
  중앙대 문학상, 한국농민문학상, 동국대 동국문학상
  서울 서초문학상, 한국생활문학회 대상 국무총리 표창

- 포상(국가 훈장, 포장, 표창)
  황조근정훈장, 근정포장
  대통령표창, 국무총리표창

- 저서
  윌리엄 워즈워드의 자연관 외 12권
  학술논문 : 윌트 휘트먼의 인간과 외 34편

- 번역서
  톰 존슨의 모험 ; 헨리필딩
  허영의 시장 ; 윌리엄 메이크피스 쌔커리,
  로버트 브라우닝 명시선, 위리엄 워즈의 명시선 외 15권
  정찬우 시집 ;「내 영혼의 하얀 미소」 외 6권

About the translator : HONGKYU Augustine CHOE

Education ; Chung-Ang University BA
Seoul National University MA
Dongguk University Ph.D

- Poet Essayist, Literary Critic, Translator
- Proficient in English, French, and German
- Professor, Professor emeritus ; Chung-Ang Unoversity, Seoul Korea

• Fullbright Exchange Professor ;
  - Yale University, Harvard University, USA
  - University of Cambridge, University of London UK
    Invited Professor
  - University of Paris IV (Sorbonne) France
  - Munchen University, German Visiting Professor

• President ; - The Korea Society for Literature and Religion
  - Pronotion Member of the Overseas Korea Literature of the Korea Writers Association
  - Committee of Welfare the Korea Writers Association ;
  - International PEN Foundation of Korea Represenrative
  - The Korea Poet's Association ; Standing Committee Member

• Awards ;
  - Epi-podo Award (English Poems, USA)
  - PEN Translation Award (Korea Center)
  - Hemingway Literary Award (Korea)
  - The Nongmin Literature Society of Korea

• National Doceration, Order, Commendation ;
  - Geunjeong Hunjang(drder), Geunjeong Pojang
  - President Commendation, Prime Minister Commendation

• Translator ;
  - Tom Jones by Henry Fielding
  - Vanity Fair by William Makepeace Thackeray
  - Selected Poems by Willam Wordswoth
  - A Fascinating Journey by Chan-Woo Chung and fifteen book
  - Translated 32 book of novel, essay

달빛에 띄운 연정(戀情)
Love in the Moonlight

인　쇄 | 2023년 7월 24일
발　행 | 2023년 7월 25일

지은이 | 정찬우
번　역 | 최홍규
펴낸곳 | 도서출판 밀레

등　록 | 2004년 12월 15일 제204078호
주　소 | 서울 서초구 효령로 53길 18, 210호
(서초동, 석탑오피스텔)
TEL : (02)588-4671~2
FAX : (02)588-4673
e-mail : hyunwoot@hanmail.net

값 20,000원
ISBN 978-89-97815-29-6